#iBetOnMe

#iBetOnMe

THE POWER of SELF-MOTIVATION

DONTE' DAVIS

#iBetOnMe: THE POWER OF SELF-MOTIVATION

© Copyright 2019 — Donte Davis

All rights reserved. This book is protected under the copyright laws of the United States. No part of this publication may be reproduced, stored in a retrieval system or transmitted in any form or by any means, including electronic, mechanical, photocopying, recording or otherwise, without the prior written permission of the copyright owner, except by a reviewer, who may quote brief passages in a review.

This book may not be copied or reprinted for commercial gain or profit. The use of short quotations is permitted and encouraged.

Interior and cover design by LifeVoiceQuest.com

ISBN: 978-0-578-47891-3

For worldwide distribution. Printed in the United States.

Contents

Author
Preface

Season One: Manifest *13*

Season Two: Testimony *37*

Season Three: Wisdom *61*

Season Four: Temptation *85*

Season Five: Frustration *109*

Season Six: Serenity *133*

Thank You

Author

My name is Donte' Davis, I'm a father, husband, Men's college basketball coach, business owner and author.

I am the creator and owner of a motivational brand entitled Manifest Excellence Inc.

When I created this brand my soul purpose was to help empower anyone who has ever second guessed reaching their definition of success. I've lived by a motto that asks a specific question: "If I don't know how to motivate myself, how can I look to other for motivation when they don't have a clue what I'm battling?" This journey began when I was given the opportunity to coach and teach high school boys the game of basketball. That opportunity metastasized into an unstoppable manifestation to reach a goal no one thought I could—coaching at the division one university level. l always envisioned myself motivating young men to be the best student athletes they could be.

With my writing I can now take that vision and empower as many people as I can simply with what influenced me to achieve the unachievable.

www.Manifestexcellenceme.org

Instagram.com/donted04w

Instagram.com/ibetonme

Twitter.com/Coachdontedavis

Preface

The word (manifest) is the underline purpose of not just my book, but my blog, website and journey. What I manifested drove me to sacrifice more than I'd ever thought, It forced me to work harder than I knew and it tightened my focus that developed into obsession. Its why we are talking today, so hello to everyone who has taken the time to read my thoughts, navigate through my journey while sharing every inch of your journey with me, this book is entirely interactive.

After every quote there will be my thoughts and questions I asked myself, now ill be asking you. This book will allow you to interact with not just me, but yourself. Jot down everything that comes to mind, use those thoughts to develop your identity towards what it is you're in pursuit of. Those actions follow my blueprint, I found great joy in talking with myself, challenging myself and motivating myself. If we can not self-motivate how can we develop the drive to become motivated by someone else's words who has no idea what were battling, overcoming or what we are in pursuit of? That's why this book is entitled 'The POWER of self-motivation'. The structure was built way before the blueprint, its up to us to not only find the blueprint, but abide by it. Every win, loss, failure and success, were supposed to see it through.

Each season (chapter) is a microcosm of the days, weeks and months that develop from the beginning to the end of our journey. Progression doesn't happen overnight, it doesn't happen tomorrow, or the next day. True progression happens a week from now or two weeks from now when our sole focus isn't on reaching our manifestation. Progression happens when we feel like quitting because of all the obstacles thrown our way, yet we stay vigilant and remain dedicated to our goal. Over a season of discipline, focus and determination, we will positively progress exactly how were expected. Welcome to the beginning, I hope you not only learn a lot about what helped me, but I hope you also develop the thoughts that create actions to what will help you achieve your goals.

SEASON 1

Man·i·fest:

Clear or obvious to the eye or mind.

SEASON 1 // MANIFEST

"There is no competition when you're manifesting your own lane." — Unknown

What do we manifest? What is so clear to our eye or mind that it drives us and consumes all of our time? What manifestation have we had that wouldn't allow us to rest until we accomplished it? Those thoughts and ideas can't be taken from us, its like the godly creation of a child, no one can argue or dispute with their parents, the child they've helped create only involves two people. Our manifestations only come to life when we take the time to birth them. That's creating our own lane, taking what we have manifested and develop the ways to make it real. No one can alter how fast were traveling or how many speed bumps there are if no one knows where we going?

SEASON 1 // MANIFEST

"Our manifestations only come to life when we take the time to birth them."

THOUGHTS

SEASON 1 // MANIFEST

"Working on myself, by myself, for myself. — Unknown

What's the premise behind bettering ourselves? Some of us think that the leap of faith is for us as an individual. Yet if we have children, significant others or family who are depending on us, we aren't soaring throughout those clouds alone. Bettering ourselves motivates, inspires and drives the people around us.

When I began organizing this book, my daughter then decided to write and then my wife as well. And now I have a few other friends that want to become authors, so they've invested in being counseled by me about the steps. What we create becomes part of our legacy. Just as what we do when given the time we're awarded on this earth. We may be bettering ourselves by ourselves, but it affects everyone around us. Are we ready to take on that responsibility?

SEASON 1 // MANIFEST

"Bettering ourselves motivates, inspires and drives the people around us."

THOUGHTS

SEASON 1 // MANIFEST

"Hold the vision, trust the process." — *Unknown*

When manifesting a vision, the progression takes time. How do we hold on to those desires to achieve? Making the completion of that goal a priority in our lives secures any thought of losing track of or mishandling those thoughts or progressions.

Reaching a goal takes a certain level of obsession—if it's a true goal there isn't anything that will alter our focus. We have to be vigilant and relentless while in pursuit. If we aren't, the percentage of us achieving the ultimate goal dwindles just as our focus does. How do we hold onto our vision and what do we do that allows us to trust the process?

"If it's a true goal there isn't anything that will alter our focus."

THOUGHTS

SEASON 1 // MANIFEST

"You are responsible for your happiness. In fact, you create it. You manifest it." — Unknown

What is our individual definition of what makes us happy? What are the steps we're consistently taking to obtain what we define as happiness? If we can't successfully answer those questions, how can we say we're in pursuit of happiness? Do we truly want it? It's like saying we want to lose weight without working out or saying we desire to learn more yet we don't seek out knowledge.

We are fully responsible for our past, present and future happiness. There's only one way to obtain what we define it as—what are we doing daily to create and pursue that definition? Never relinquish that power to others—that will be the second we begin to regret not being in control of our own happiness.

SEASON 1 // MANIFEST

"We are fully responsible for our past, present and future happiness."

THOUGHTS

SEASON 1 // MANIFEST

"Speak as if it already exists. Act as if it's already yours." — Unknown

In order to believe in the dream, we must know we are worthy of living it. I speak from experience. I spoke so much life into accomplishing my goal that when it happened it wasn't as big of a surprise to me as it was to others.

We have to know where we're going. That is what's in the cards. We have to respect what we manifest so much that we foolishly take a leap of faith to accomplish it. Just as we sike ourselves out of pursuing a goal we have to trick our minds into thinking were on such a path that there's no doubt we will achieve it. Before you achieved your goal what was your mentality?

SEASON 1 // MANIFEST

"In order to believe in the dream, we must know we are worthy of living it."

THOUGHTS

SEASON 1 // MANIFEST

"Change the way you think and you change your life."
— *Unknown*

How many of us go into a new year contemplating getting rid of all the things we believe are detrimental to our lives? What if our mentality is the only trait we need to alter? We argue with ourselves about the people we have around. We ponder about the things we watch or even the food we ingest, yet how many of us focus on our mental health?

Some of us aren't where we want to be simply because of us. We can be our worst enemy, nitpicking at every reason why we shouldn't. But we could also convince ourselves that there's no other way than chasing our dreams. Is that something we've tried, and are we conscious enough to know just how much our mentality plays into our personal success?

SEASON 1 // MANIFEST

"We can be our worst enemy nitpicking at every reason why we shouldn't, but we could also convince ourselves that there's no other way than chasing our dreams."

THOUGHTS

SEASON 1 // MANIFEST

"Don't call it a dream, call it a plan." — *Unknown*

When I decided to risk it all, everyone kept saying to me, "You know, not all dreams can be a reality, right?" My rebuttal? "I'm not chasing a dream, I'm executing my plan." Of course, that's where the conversation ended. Most of those people smiled and then called me crazy. Some laughed and said, "Good luck." Yet very few walked closer, looked around, then asked, "What's your plan?" I hung onto every inch of their advice.

The few were the people who have once been in my shoes and wanted to make sure I didn't torture myself just as they did. When I achieved my goal, those were the first people I reached out to ... to express my gratitude. What we are chasing isn't a dream. Understand the only way it becomes reality is with elite planning. We will be wrong some of the time. We will have to double back and alter the plan. Yet stay invested. It's our plan. What leads up to the completion of the journey is what matters the most. How would we rate our planning?

SEASON 1 // MANIFEST

"I'm not chasing a dream, I'm executing my plan."

THOUGHTS

SEASON 1 // MANIFEST

"You don't need to be great to start. You don't need to start to be great." — Unknown

As a men's college basketball coach, it took me too long to sit down, focus and believe I could not only write my book, but start my brand. I truly believed that if I started this I wouldn't be able to do anything else. This is false. I talked myself out of doing something I have an immense passion for.

Having the opportunity to talk to a plethora of people about their journey is exciting. I didn't have anyone to discuss what I manifested so I was navigating through my journey, confident yet blindfolded. When I decided to begin this book I thought of all the people who are currently in the same boat I was in. Having someone to talk to about what others may say is impossible or crazy helps to add fuel to the internal burning fire.

SEASON 1 // MANIFEST

"I truly believed that if I started this I wouldn't be able to do anything else."

THOUGHTS

SEASON 1 // MANIFEST

"Do not ask the Lord to guide your footsteps if you are not willing to move your feet." — Unknown

I am a Christian. I do believe in a Higher Power, so when I speak of betting on "ME," I am also putting all my eggs in the basket of the God I love and trust to guide my life. For the people who do believe, we pray, beg and ask for guidance. We plead to have another shot when we fail. We even look for signs to be shown when we don't have a clue.

Yet why ask if we aren't willing to do our part? No one will reach their definition of success by doing nothing. Do we want success? We cannot run from the work it takes to achieve it. How much work are we willing to put in to reach the top of our mountain?

SEASON 1 // MANIFEST

"No one will reach their definition of success by doing nothing. You want success? You cannot run from the work it takes to achieve it."

THOUGHTS

SEASON 1 // MANIFEST

"Fill your life with experiences, not things. Have stories to tell, not stuff to show." — Unknown

When I decided to begin this journey I had no idea what all would come with it. I didn't know how to maneuver through or what I would do the closer I got to achieving my goal. The one thing I did know is wherever it took me, I would appreciate it and learn from every experience. This game of basketball has taken me all over the world. It has allowed me to meet some of the most genuine, smart, humble, connected and determined people I've ever known.

No matter what the outcome, that's the one thing besides what I've learned that can't be taken nor quantified: my experiences. The places I've been, the knowledge I've accumulated, along with the people God has placed in my life ... I'll take all of those experiences over anything material that I've been able to purchase every day of the week. What are the things we're cherishing throughout our journey?

SEASON 1 // MANIFEST

"No matter what the outcome, that's the one thing, besides what I've learned, that can't be taken nor quantified: my experiences."

THOUGHTS

END OF SEASON 1

The manifest season is incredibly vital to everyone's development. Without it, there's no journey. Season One should display not only the ability to recognize our manifestations, but it should also create alternate realities that show us we can make them actuality. Lastly, it should stir up our desire to want to create those plans that inch us closer and closer every day until we're living that very manifestation.

Every journey has a beginning. Our manifestations can't start anywhere but in-between our ears. The second we want to act upon those manifestations is the second our lifelong journey to bettering ourselves begins. Did we take the challenge? Now that we're ingratiated in our manifestation, how does it feel? Where do we go from here? What's next? Take on those questions with our head raised high, our confidence dialed up to a thousand, and willingness to turn our humility up. "Why," we ask? Its testimony time, that's why. With every stage of growth, we won't be prepared. Because its growth, no one is fully ready for what comes with it.

SEASON 2

Tes·ti·mo·ny:

A formal written or spoken statement.

SEASON 2 // TESTIMONY

"You will either step forward into growth, or you will step back into safety." — Unknown

Welcome to Season Two. I assume we've decided to step into growth versus staying in our comfort zone. Yes, this season will be blurry, filled with uncertainty and nervousness. Yet those are the traits identified as growth. Embrace them, trust them and focus on overcoming. Just as manifestations are vital to our development, so is season two. Everyone has a testimony. Most don't want to share. Some desire for people to listen. Which one are we?

SEASON 2 // TESTIMONY

"Yes this season will be blurry, filled with uncertainty and nervousness. Yet those are the traits identified as growth. Embrace them, trust them and focus on overcoming."

THOUGHTS

SEASON 2 // TESTIMONY

"The future lies before you, like paths of pure white snow. Be careful how you treat it, for every step will show." — Unknown

Every day we pursue a goal. Most of us are equipped with tunnel vision, exclusively focusing on where we're going yet neglecting where we've come from. Take the time to turn around and admire the footsteps you've created. There will be some steps we aren't happy about. Yet those very steps allow us to be where we are today.

We have to be cognizant of not just what we learn, but what we're leaving behind. They aren't just steps. They are mistakes, pain, hurt, joy, success … but most importantly, they are lessons. With those experiences, we are molded into who we are. Without those lessons, we wouldn't transform into the person who is prepared for not just success, but the next challenge that's being presented. Just how much are we cherishing those steps?

SEASON 2 // TESTIMONY

"We have to be cognizant of not just what we learn, but what we're leaving behind."

THOUGHTS

SEASON 2 // TESTIMONY

"Testimony is to know and feel. Conversion is to do and to become." — Unknown

How do we feel when someone asks us to talk about our testimony? How willing are we to express some of the emotions and thoughts that created the person we are today? We all want to be the ones who proclaim reaching our goals by ourselves -- no one helped us, we did this all alone. In reality, we all need people to help guide us, tell us the truth, scold us for not staying focused and even someone that's smarter than us.

That's why I love the word testimony. It opens the door to sharing ideas and motivations that can and will spark the minds of others. Most of the time this will come back to us. When it comes back, it consistently challenges our thoughts and viewpoints. This isn't exclusively about the people we trust and love. I've grown exponentially through people who were negative and challenged every inch of my thoughts. I strongly believe that's what fueled my fire —knowing this challenge was impossible, knowing people didn't understand what I was pursuing. They were all about conversation. There were no actions they could take to alter this journey. Know and feel versus conversation ... which one drives us?

SEASON 2 // TESTIMONY

"We all want to be the ones who proclaim reaching our goals by ourselves. No one helped us, we did this all alone."

THOUGHTS

SEASON 2 // TESTIMONY

"Fear can keep us up all night, but faith makes one fine pillow." — Unknown

If fear supposedly keeps us up all night, why are we so well rested? Since it's taken us so long to take that first step, we've been sleeping to past the time. I don't know about you, yet that's what took me so long to begin my journey—nervousness, second-guessing my commitment and being fearful about succeeding.

Why are we so in fear about what we say we want? Is it because we love the idea of achieving the goal, the lifestyle that comes with that type of success. Or is it because we don't have a clue how to handle success? What answers all of those hesitations is faith. Having the confidence in ourselves and faith in a Higher Power will give us all the calm we need to take that leap of faith. Even if we don't believe in a Higher Power, we must have faith in ourselves that what we've manifested is the right move for us. How fine is our faith pillow?

SEASON 2 // TESTIMONY

"Why are we so in fear of what we say we want?"

THOUGHTS

SEASON 2 // TESTIMONY

"You will never know your limits unless you push yourself to them." — *Unknown*

I love the word "limits"- a point or level beyond which something does NOT or may NOT extend or pass. The capital/bold word is why I love it so much. What does that word do to us? When I'm in pursuit of a goal I keep that word really close to me. If I ever have a day where I think I've made it, I read the definition and I'm ready to work. If we truly believe there are limitations, then that's the reason we aren't where we should be. When we make the conscious decision to take that leap, we should focus more on how to stay afloat and how we can fly higher than if we can fly at all.

SEASON 2 // TESTIMONY

"If we truly believe there are limitations, then that's the reason we aren't where we should be."

THOUGHTS

SEASON 2 // TESTIMONY

"I'm not normal. I don't want to be. I don't pretend to be. It's quite simple, I am me." — Unknown

The most successful people in the world correlate insanity to success. I believe that correlation 100%. We have to be borderline insane to not only think we can accomplish something that far in our view, not to mention taking a leap of faith knowing there is a possibility that we could fall. Yet that's where having the confidence of one hundred people and faith stronger than the strongest person in the world comes in.

We need to have that mentality that we aren't normal. Here's a little secret: there's nothing wrong with being "different", that's what makes us unique. How does the saying go— what you eat don't make me sh*t? Have that same focus pertaining to accomplishing a goal. Just because others won't, can't and don't, doesn't mean we can't. Don't allow anyone to put their limitations onto you. When you make the decision to pursue it, don't stop until you achieve it.

SEASON 2 // TESTIMONY

"We need to have that mentality that we aren't normal: Here's a little secret: there's nothing wrong with being 'different,' that's what makes us unique."

THOUGHTS

SEASON 2 // TESTIMONY

"There is nothing in the world that can trouble you more than your own thoughts." — Unknown

When talking to people about the meaning of my brand, I always ask about their journey. I stress to them that goals with concrete limitations (high school, college) are the easiest to accomplish. Why? Because no matter how we do it, educators are telling us, if we take these specific classes we will graduate with our high school diploma and/or college degree.

If we can't be mentally tough enough to accomplish a goal that has a distinctive requirement, how would we tackle the beast of starting a business, writing a script or anything that requires the unknown variable of time? Don't allow our thoughts to be the blame for not being happy. Just as we had the ability to manifest that goal, we can also turn it into reality. It just takes the time that we didn't view within that manifestation.

SEASON 2 // TESTIMONY

"If we can't be mentally tough enough to accomplish a goal that has a distinctive requirement, how would we tackle the beast of starting a business, writing a script or anything that requires the unknown variable of time?"

THOUGHTS

SEASON 2 // TESTIMONY

"Recovery brought my head out of my ass. Just for today I no longer live in a world of shit." — Unknown

How many of us believe we can possibly be the reason why we aren't where we should be? If we are arrogant within our pursuit, we can unfortunately block our own blessings. Who's heard that before? For the people who identify, what were some of your recovery actions you've taken to not only keep yourself humble but learn from that arrogance?

There are quite a few of us who developed the haughtiness trait once we stumbled upon gaining an extra inch of progress we didn't see coming. It would be advantageous for those accomplishments. No one enjoys living in a world full of filth, there are two key words that will add substantial worth to our journey: humility and patience. Remaining humble is a vital trait to have when transforming into a new person. Yes, we are changing ... yet how we act and react can be the reason we gain another inch toward our goal. Or it could be the reason why we take five steps backward. Patience allows us to understand we will not accomplish everything overnight. It will take time. If we don't realize reality, it will deter us from opening any doors that we need.

SEASON 2 // TESTIMONY

"If we are arrogant within our pursuit, we can unfortunately block our own blessings."

THOUGHTS

"Be grateful for today and never take anything for granted. Life is a blessing." — Unknown

The first task I tackle when I wake up is prayer—I want to thank the man above for giving me another opportunity to be a husband, father, mentor, coach, son, and brother. There are a plethora of simple things in life that allow us the mobility to do what it is we say we want to do. If we can't cherish the little things how would we appreciate the major accomplishment (or failures) in life?

Remaining humble and grateful will add so much positive energy and blessings for anyone and their pursuit. What are we appreciative of? What don't we take for granted? What part of our journey do/did we appreciate the most? Do we understand just how much of a blessing it is when granted another day of life? Or do we think it's supposed to happen? I tell all my players at the beginning of the season, "Take a deep breath." We don't know how many more of those we will get, so cherish every single one—just as I want us to cherish the opportunity we have to attend college (for free) and play the game we love.

SEASON 2 // TESTIMONY

"There are a plethora of simple things in life that allow us the mobility to do what it is we say we want to do."

THOUGHTS

SEASON 2 // TESTIMONY

"Never give up on a dream just because of the time it will take to accomplish it." — Unknown

How many of us have manifested a goal, spoke life into it, shared our testimony, and then didn't take that leap of faith simply because the distance of the journey frightened us? My hand is raised with you. I've felt that exact same way you're feeling right now. The difference? I closed my eyes, took a deep breath, then prayed. The second I came to, there was an unstoppable force in my feet, a determination in my eyes ... and then I took the leap.

I knew I'd be soaring above and within the clouds. I knew I ingratiated myself into a journey I never encountered before, yet I embraced it. The ability to commit will positively alter your life for the better. Never give up on what it is you've manifested. The time it takes to accomplish your goal may look long, yet enjoy every step of the journey.

SEASON 2 // TESTIMONY

"I knew I'd be soaring above and within the clouds, I knew I ingratiated myself into a journey I never encountered before, yet I embraced it."

THOUGHTS

END OF SEASON 2

Just how important do we think our testimony is? I hope we've come to the realization after season two that it's important! As Season Two comes to the end, what are our thoughts about it? What type of person are we? Are we the type that dislikes sharing our thoughts and ideas with others (for whatever reason), or are we the one that obtains more information and inspiration from sharing our testimony?

Whichever one we are, this book suits both parties. Having an interactive book allows the reader to not only read great content that sparks their thoughts, it gives them the availability to write those ideas down so they stay fresh. Our testimony is just as important as our manifestation—if we verbalize it, we see it; if we consistently see it, that will give us a greater chance to achieve it. Allowing our testimony to be someone's wisdom will inspire more people than we think.

SEASON 3

Words of Wis·dom

The quality of having experience, knowledge, and good judgment, the quality of being wise.

SEASON 3 // WORDS OF WISDOM

"Take what you have and use it to create what you want." — Unknown

Access to knowledge today has altered the world as we know it. There isn't anything we shouldn't know seeing that the information is so accessible. So taking what we have to create what we want should be easy correct? What puts a halt to that progression is the desire to want to obtain that information.

If we want to create a business, there are videos we could research and watch that will give us step by step instructions on how to do so. There are even a plethora of motivational speakers that could assist us to get out of our own way to achieve the unachievable. There's nothing that can stop us. We are the most celebrated person and negative alley in our circle that could alter our success. So if we need instructions on how to find ways to obtain knowledge, then we don't want it bad enough. Take what you have (which is everything) to obtain what you want. That's why wisdom is one of the key seasons for our journey. Without it, we just have a dream and words. Yet if the sharing of your testimony consistently sparks ideas, then you're on your way to recycling that act which will always refresh your thoughts.

SEASON 3 // WORDS OF WISDOM

"There isn't anything we shouldn't know since that knowledge is so accessible."

THOUGHTS

SEASON 3 // WORDS OF WISDOM

"Don't let negative and toxic people rent space in your head. Raise the rent and kick them out." — *Unknown*

Do we think monitoring the people around us is as important or less important than the knowledge we're responsible to seek? There are a lot of variables that go into reaching a personal goal. Not everyone has the same desire and focus to do so. There may be people around who want to impede your motion toward success.

What do we do with those people? Understand if they aren't pouring into us, they're taking from us. I learned early on that I would lose a lot of people on my journey. It hurts. It sucks. Yet it's warranted. Not everyone is required to be present when we win—they can't handle the person we will transform into. Don't lose out on the opportunity of a lifetime because you aren't willing to be truthful about the people you allow to hang around.

SEASON 3 // WORDS OF WISDOM

"Understand if they aren't pouring into you, they're taking from you."

THOUGHTS

> *"Life is change. Growth is optional. Choose wisely."*
> *— Unknown*

If we have a difficult time adapting to change, how would we ever grow? Committing to reaching our goals requires us to change. Who we are today won't be who we are throughout the journey and especially not at the end. The question is how much will we grow throughout that experience. We will all develop over time but are we focusing on growing every time our life changes?

Growth is understanding the mistakes we've made and not making them again. Growth is not just navigating through but intentionally taking every step only to gain that infamous inch. So what's most important to us? Living a life of change or growing within life?

SEASON 3 // WORDS OF WISDOM

"Growth is understanding the mistakes we've made and not making them again. Growth is not just navigating through but intentionally taking every step only to gain that infamous inch."

THOUGHTS

SEASON 3 // WORDS OF WISDOM

"When everything feels like an uphill struggle, just think of the view from the top." — Unknown

Who's currently on that hill, feet dug in, fingers scraping the gravel, tightly holding on, out of breath, wiping the sweat out our eyes and questioning if continuing to climb is worth it? There will be more than one day where we don't want to improve. There will be WEEKS where we feel like we have time and everything will be okay. Those are the days that hurt us the most.

Ease and comfort are more detrimental to progress than never deciding to start our journey at all. Those are the days we keep the dirt in our eyes, allow the tears to stream down our faces, embrace just how much pain we're enduring. We focus on nothing but the top of that mountain. These days are the days that truly develop and add so much more growth to our progress than we equate. When it hurts to stand and when we're too tired to keep going … that's the time to focus. Focus on not just why we started, but why we're currently thriving on the side of this mountain.

SEASON 3 // WORDS OF WISDOM

"Ease and comfort are more detrimental to progress than never deciding to start our journey at all."

THOUGHTS

SEASON 3 // WORDS OF WISDOM

"When we learn to accept instead of except, you will have fewer disappointments." — Unknown

Accepting the path God had planned for me wasn't difficult. Committing to that path was. The second I decided to accept the path, I knew I made the right decision. I also knew I would have to no longer accept my excuses, my hesitation or my fears. That's the true starting point of our journey, accepting our paths.

If we don't accept our manifestations, there will be no testimony nor the development of wisdom. Stop accepting the negative thoughts, the fears of our peers and the second-guessing that creep into our minds. Accept the challenge and never use accept as a reason for coming up short again.

SEASON 3 // WORDS OF WISDOM

"If we don't accept our manifestations, there will be no testimony nor the development of wisdom."

THOUGHTS

> "A comfort zone is a beautiful place, but nothing ever grows there." — Unknown

How many of us are so ingratiated in our day to day routine that we lose sight of how to effectively grow? We're so locked into comfort that we don't give any thought to deviating from that mentality. The zone of comfortability can hinder our journey. I use a massive Godly creation like a mountain as a metaphor for our journey because that's what a manifestation is—a mental creation that God has blessed us with. Once we claw our way to the top of our mountain, will we sit back and relax, or will we look in the distance, spot another mountain, climb down and begin our journey to conquer yet another task?

If innovation or groundbreaking creation came from a comfort state, there would be less trial and error and more success. In order to grow and improve, we must step out of our comfort zone. The state of being uncomfortable should become comfortable. There's nothing like learning from our mistakes, understanding our path and figuring out how to make our manifestations come to life. When we become uncomfortable, that's when our positive progression begins.

SEASON 3 // WORDS OF WISDOM

"In order to grow and improve we must step out of our comfort zone. The state of being uncomfortable should become comfortable."

THOUGHTS

> "Life will only change when we become more committed to our dreams than we are to our comfort zone." — Unknown

How many of us credit our success to a certain level of commitment? If we've had any success in our lives (I know all of us have) then we all should give credit to ourselves. That's where we develop most of our wisdom. Understanding just how committed we were pushed us to block out all distractions and focus solely on reaching our goal ... that is the solid base we need to begin.

Being committed to our manifestations will be the driving force to saying we achieved, or I wish I would have. When we are dedicated to achieving a goal we have to come to terms with how much we will sacrifice, how much time it takes. But most importantly we must realize just how far we have to step away from our comfort zone.

SEASON 3 // WORDS OF WISDOM

"Being committed to our manifestations will be the driving force to saying you achieved, or I wish I would have."

THOUGHTS

"The invariable mark of wisdom is to see the miraculous in the common." — Unknown

What's something we view as insignificant that could make a major impact in our life/journey? Mine was writing, I began to jot down what was on my mind pertaining to my goal of becoming a division one men's basketball coach. That gave me the ability to visualize what my moves could be and the moves that were deemed mistakes. When we begin to see what we are thinking, that allows us to understand what our calling is.

Just as a lot of you, when I took my leap of faith, I didn't have a clue if I'd hit the ground. All I knew was I wanted to coach at that level more than anything. I also learned the value of consistent communication. When I began talking to college coaches I realized we had so much in common that those conversations transformed into friendships and brotherhoods. I was building relationships with people who are not just in the field that I desire, they've been thriving there for years. All I needed was positive mentorship willing to give me as much wisdom as I yearned for. My desire to seek wisdom displayed what we had in common. This opened the door to me being able to reach my goal. What if wisdom is the common denominator to why we haven't reached our goals?

SEASON 3 // WORDS OF WISDOM

"What if wisdom is the common denominator to why we haven't reached our goals?"

THOUGHTS

SEASON 3 // WORDS OF WISDOM

"Most of the most important things in the world have been accomplished by people who kept on trying when there seemed to be no hope at all." — Unknown

What would have to happen in our life for us to never stop pursuing the goal we've manifested? When we look around, everything we see took tons of time to create. What if those people gave up? What if those people decided the pity they're feeling is more important then completing their creation? A creation that could not only could change their lives but could change the world?

What would happen if the single creation we needed that assisted us to continue to create didn't exist due to someone's inability to stay mentally strong? What if that person is us? What if what we've manifested could change our lives and possibly help inspire someone else? I'm here to tell you it is, what you've manifested will change your life. It may not inspire others, yet the act of taking your leap of faith that leads to you accomplishing your goal might be the only action others need to see.

SEASON 3 // WORDS OF WISDOM

"What would happen if the single creation we needed that assisted us to continue to create didn't exist due to someone giving in to their inability to stay mentally strong?"

THOUGHTS

SEASON 3 // WORDS OF WISDOM

"Maturity is not when we start speaking big things. It is when we start understanding small things."
— Unknown

Throughout our journey, we have to understand there will be times where the signs sit motionless right in front of us, and there are other times (more times than not) that the signs will be the little things that some of us don't notice. How many times have we walked by something or read a book or even heard a song and didn't notice something small that actually means more than everything else we're hearing or seeing? The reason why we don't notice it is because at those moments we aren't mature enough to recognize the little things.

When we hear the word "wisdom" we automatically think someone (or something) will give us the answers we're searching for. I'm here to tell you that's not always the case. When we are blessed to obtain wisdom, understanding what's being said to us is the most vital piece of information. Not searching for the answer to the DaVinci Code, but listening to someone who cares about us and our journey enough to give knowledge where someone else might not have that opportunity. That's why they say, "Little things come in big packages." A blessings weight can't be quantified, yet when used properly, its weight could change everything.

SEASON 3 // WORDS OF WISDOM

"How many times have we walked by something or read a book or even heard a song and didn't notice something small that actually means more than everything else we're hearing or seeing?"

THOUGHTS

END OF SEASON 3

As we come to yet another end of a great season, just how much did we learn from the importance of seeking wisdom? To give wisdom we must obtain wisdom. Having that circle of knowledge will assist more people than we know.

I once read a statement by a great coach that spoke about never allowing your free hand to display the blessings your strong hand is giving. That statement spoke volumes, especially in this day and age we all are tempted to show off our good deeds. Sadly, we also desire a great deal of praise to be attached, so is it truly a good deed?

Seeking wisdom was the most important piece to my journey. I was tempted to do things on my own, you know, carve my own lane, yet that temptation deteriorated. My path was paved as my humility increased. Have we ever been tempted to deter from the wisdom we were given?

SEASON 4

Temp·ta·tion

The desire to do something, especially something wrong or unwise.

SEASON 4 // TEMPTATION

> *"One of the greatest temptations in life is to settle for less than your worth."* — Unknown

We all have regrets in life. Some hurt worst than others, yet they still hurt. If you've reached a goal, think back to that pivotal moment where you developed that urge to take that leap. Imagine if you blinked and were still standing there, emotionless. How bad would that hurt? There are people who haven't experience that weightless feeling soaring through the sky, with the wind slightly taking their breath away, mind rambling, struggling to get a grasp of what they've done and what's next. They haven't looked left, then panned to their right to see no one but clouds. There are people who then begin to talk to themselves building confidence like never before and then snap out of it, just to notice they are holding up all their body weight with their own legs.

At that moment if we sit down and refuse to pursue that orgasmic feeling, we are settling for less than we deserve. Is the urge to sit down to understand what just happened more important than finding that cliff so we can experience it in real time?

SEASON 4 // TEMPTATION

"If you've reached a goal, think back to that pivotal moment where you developed that urge to take that leap. Imagine if you blinked and were still standing there, emotionless. How bad would that hurt?"

THOUGHTS

SEASON 4 // TEMPTATION

"When you flee from temptation, be sure you do not leave a forwarding address behind." — Unknown

When I went through a tough break up, I gave her my new cell phone number and new address. Every traumatic situation I've been through I always tattoo what happened and its location on my skin so I never forget. Sound crazy doesn't it? Is that how insane we sound when we fail and still find a way to latch on to what caused us to fail?

There are some people who can't become who they're destined to be simply because of their inability to unlatch themselves from the very things that cause them unfathomable harm. The second we decide where we're headed means more than where we've come from—that is the second our true progression begins.

SEASON 4 // TEMPTATION

"Is that how insane we sound when we fail and still find a way to latch on to what caused us to fall?"

THOUGHTS

SEASON 4 // TEMPTATION

"The road to success is dotted with many tempting parking places." — Unknown

Why do we always want the parking spot that's convenient for us? Is it because it's our lucky parking spot? Is it because the lines are straighter and we love the way it looks? Or is it because our name is written on it? None of the above is right. We want the close parking spot because it's close.

What if every time something amusing stood in a distance of our vision it would take us twice as long to get to where we're headed. The journey requires discipline, focus, trust, and belief. We can't jump at every situation that comes our way. If we allow anything or anyone to deter us from that path, that's the second we settle for less than what we're worth.

SEASON 4 // TEMPTATION

"The journey requires discipline, focus, trust, and belief."

THOUGHTS

SEASON 4 // TEMPTATION

"It is better to take many small steps in the right direction than to make a great leap forward only to stumble backward." — *Unknown*

There's not a greater feeling than progress at the end of the night. No matter how much of that inch we've gathered, as long as we've taken adequate steps towards our goal we should sleep well. The trick is consistently finding new ways to acquire those steps towards the completion of our journey. When we stumble upon opportunities that disguise themselves as a quicker path to that goal is where the discipline and focus settle in. So I ask ... is the timing of completing a goal the most important thing?

SEASON 4 // TEMPTATION

"Is the timing of completing a goal the most important thing?"

THOUGHTS

SEASON 4 // TEMPTATION

"There is nothing either good or bad. But thinking makes it so." — Unknown

When I began my pursuit it took me days to complete certain tasks simply because I talked myself out of staying focused. How many of us are guilty of that? Thinking can positively cater to or negatively ruin any pursuit of progress. Understanding how powerful our thoughts are can be allow us to focus on thinking positive thoughts along with being our own biggest fan.

Knowing how to positively champion ourselves distracts us from searching for toxic acceptance from other people. How many of us think that managing our thoughts is important? If we're more focused on our mental health, then the percentages of allowing something negative to creep in decreases. Success and our mental health ... do they go hand in hand?

SEASON 4 // TEMPTATION

"Understanding how powerful our thoughts are can allow us to focus on thinking positive thoughts along with being our own biggest fan."

THOUGHTS

SEASON 4 // TEMPTATION

"Look for something positive in each day. Even if some days you have to look a little harder." — Unknown

How many of us have come to the end of a day and struggle to find something positive about our day? What are some of the positives you look for that are on your list? Every day that I'm given the opportunity to live is a positive one. Everything that happens in-between me waking up and going to bed are experiences that add worth to my life (in every area) and my path to success.

There will be a lot of trial and error days. There also numerous days I feel invincible. Yet the days that grow us up the most are the negative ones. Those days challenge just how bad we want to succeed. If we can look ourselves in the mirror and call a failed day a success, that is when we're truly progressing.

SEASON 4 // TEMPTATION

"Every day that I'm given the opportunity to live is a positive one. Everything that happens in-between me waking up and going to bed are experiences that add worth to my life (in every area) and my path to success."

THOUGHTS

SEASON 4 // TEMPTATION

"Life doesn't come with instructions. You may make mistakes, but you live and learn." — Unknown

Who has a firm grip on life, who's shooting one hundred percent from the field on decisions made, who's learned less but lived more? None of us have, which means making it this far into the book possible. Since we understand no one in life is perfect, there shouldn't be anyone who believes they are perfectly navigating through their life or journey.

Every day we wake up there isn't a manual laying on the nightstand patiently waiting for us to read it, digest it then prepare to execute today's game plan. What if there was? What if this book served as a motivating guide that helped keep us centered throughout our day. Our journey is unique. There will be a lot of learning about the goals we're pursuing. And there will be tons of learning about ourselves. Engaging in trial and error develops us as people. Taking pride in not knowing, trying things out and watching them fail or succeed develops us. The more pride we take in understanding OUR WHY, the better we will understand ourselves.

SEASON 4 // TEMPTATION

"What if this book served as a motivating guide that helped keep us centered throughout our day."

THOUGHTS

SEASON 4 // TEMPTATION

"When tempted to fight fire with fire, remember that the fire department usually uses water." — Unknown

Think of a time we fought anger, hate or even rebellion with the very thing that's trying desperately to knock us off our path. Where did that get us? What did we learn about that situation? Imagine taking all the times we've foolishly fought back with what was trying to hurt us and used the opposite. Would we have progressed further? Would our lives be different?

What if we were so conscious about not allowing anyone or anything to alter our trajectory that we didn't fight fire with fire? Instead, we searched for the nearest firehose and distinguished it the instant we saw it begin to brew. There are some people that haven't reached their goals simply because they're more into drowning out a fire with more heat which increases the flames and makes it harder to see the water hose that's sitting within reach. The more time we take not distinguishing the fire, the more damage it will cause to what we've built.

SEASON 4 // TEMPTATION

"What if we were so conscious about not allowing anyone or anything to alter our trajectory that we didn't fight fire with fire? Instead, we searched where the nearest firehose was and distinguished it the second we saw it begin to brew."

THOUGHTS

SEASON 4 // TEMPTATION

"Virtue cannot exist without temptation and difficulties to be overcome." — *Unknown*

Who has lost count of the number of tempting encounters we've come across? What age were we when we began to truly hurt when we fell victim to temptations? Who looks at temptation as a bad thing? I myself am truly thankful for tempting passions. It's made me who I am today. There's nothing like having full control over our mentality and reactions.

Analyzing the good we have in our lives, respecting how far we've traveled and the road we've paved gives us the strength to look at those tempting moments and walk away knowing it's not worth it. Especially when we've failed before. We know how difficult it is to start over and how bad we feel when we have to have that talk with ourselves. We knew it was bad. We knew it was not worth it. Sometimes those talks humble us more than anything else. What are some of the ways to positively overcome a tempting moment? How can we focus more on what all we've done that will keep us on track to not think there's a quicker way to where we're trying to go?

SEASON 4 // TEMPTATION

"Analyzing the good we have in our lives, respecting how far we've traveled and the road we've paved gives us the strength to look at those tempting moments and walk away knowing it's not worth it."

THOUGHTS

SEASON 4 // TEMPTATION

"Spare minutes are the gold dust of time, the portions of life most fruitful in good and evil, the gaps through which temptation enter." — Unknown

Besides my family, time means the most to me. How many of us have sat down and focused on what it is we do with our time? Time is just as precious as family and air. Without it, there is nothing. That's why I'll always cherish it. I try to always stay busy maintaining my relationship with my beautiful wife (happy wife happy life!). My passion as a father, my leadership as a mentor/men's college basketball coach and my discipline as a writer. My day is filled with positive progression in the most important areas of my life.

Those identifiers define who I am as a man. If I don't pour into them they will begin to deteriorate. For those who don't cherish the spare minutes of the day what have we replaced progression with? Frustration, anxiety or apprehension is a result of failing to appreciate our spare minutes. Allowing negativity to thrive within those minutes causes doubt that ultimately leads to failure. Are we allowing temptation to creep in which causes us to develop failing ways?

SEASON 4 // TEMPTATION

"My day is filled with positive progression in the most important areas of my life."

THOUGHTS

END OF SEASON 4

Welcome to the end of a great season. I believe the temptation season can be the most important topic within our journey. As someone who has fallen victim to a tempting passion, I know just how difficult it is in that moment to make the right decision. Giving solid advice and sharing our stories could help others not suffer the same failures we've endured is the premise behind this season.

We've all failed to tempting ways. Finding a way to not repeat those acts helps us become stronger ... which keeps us on our path. How did this season help us? What did it say to us and how did we receive it? If we fail to stay vigilant, frustration takes over. How well can we handle not being who we are? Let's find out in the next season. Hope we enjoyed season four. Welcome to season five.

SEASON 5

Frus·tra·tion

The feeling of being upset or annoyed,
especially because of inability to change
or achieve something.

SEASON 5 // FRUSTRATION

"Tears are often a sign of frustration." — Unknown

I knew things needed to change when I began to cry often. I knew I had to have a coming-to-God moment when I didn't notice myself in the mirror. And I knew I had to make drastic changes when nothing motivated me anymore. How many of us go through moments of our lives like this? Those identifiers described me the spring and summer of 2011. With a wife and a two-year-old daughter I should have had everything I needed to inspire me, yet I didn't.

I wasn't happy with my career choice and everyone recognized my discomfort. What are our thoughts when we wake up every day to pursue money and not our true passion? Some of us understand more than others what that feeling is like. The moment we understand we aren't fulfilling our purpose is what this book embodies. At what lengths would we travel to achieve our goals and live in our purpose?

SEASON 5 // FRUSTRATION

"What are our thoughts when we wake up every day to pursue money and not our true passion?"

THOUGHTS

SEASON 5 // FRUSTRATION

"You know its time to change your life around when you start getting frustrated and disappointed with yourself." — Unknown

When we aren't ourselves, when we begin to question everything we do or even wonder why we are here, how do we respond? Do we try to find a way to begin the process of reaching our goals? Or are we more afraid to make a move simply because we aren't directly equipped with the tools? This part of my life was the most difficult. How do we know we're making the right decision? How do we know this is the path we should take?

Those questions define my reasoning to why I started this book confessing to everyone that I'm a Christian. Having faith in who I serve allowed me to have that sense of calm and a heavy belief that whatever decision I was making he was co-signing. The moment we are at the crossroads is the moment our character shines the brightest. It's when our focus on what we've manifested is displayed. We all know what we want to do in life, we just struggle with committing to it.

SEASON 5 // FRUSTRATION

"Having faith in who I serve allowed me to have that sense of calm and a heavy belief that whatever decision I was making he was cosigning."

THOUGHTS

SEASON 5 // FRUSTRATION

"Hard times are often blessings in disguise. Let go and let life strengthen you. No matter how much it hurts, hold your head up and keep going." — Unknown

How difficult is it to let go and learn from life when we're fighting through a rough path? Who read that quote and thought, "Easier said than done." I know I did until I began this journey. There were so many hills, excruciating challenges and extremely bumpy avenues getting to where I am today. I questioned if I would make it.

Until one day I was going through it bad and I began to smile. I closed my eyes and whispered, "No matter what comes my way, I'm destroying it." I took that energy with me that day, the next day, and the following day. I finally tattooed it to my chest and in my mind that no matter what day it is, that's the energy anything and everything would feel if it tested me. I've never felt so in control, I've never felt so ready, and I've never seen clearer. I knew that was the day I had evolved into the person closest to who I'd eventually be.

SEASON 5 // FRUSTRATION

"I took that energy with me that day, the next day, and the following day. I finally tattooed it to my chest and in my mind that no matter what day it is, that's the energy anything and everything would feel if it tested me."

THOUGHTS

SEASON 5 // FRUSTRATION

"Success consists of going from failure to failure without loss of enthusiasm." — Unknown

I embrace failure. It drives me. It also gives me the reality I need to recalibrate my thoughts on the path I'm taking. How many of us pursued a goal and didn't have any doubt that it was the correct route to go? Then we failed and ended up on the path that was truly meant for us? Those are the type of failures that assist more than deter.

Don't get me wrong, a fail is a loss of effort, energy, and focus ... but most importantly TIME. Yet there isn't one successful man or woman who has reached their definition of success without some type of failure. There are different types of failures, just as there are different definitions of success. What is your definition of a failure?

SEASON 5 // FRUSTRATION

"Yet there isn't one successful man or woman who has reached their definition of success without some type of failure."

THOUGHTS

SEASON 5 // FRUSTRATION

"After failure, don't make moves without praying about it first." — Unknown

How many of us attack a goal, fail, then start to ingratiate prayer into our routine? We are all human. A lot of us do. I'm not perfect, I do it as well. Have we ever thought about including prayer into our journey before we take that leap of faith? Do we think the outcome would change?

From my experience, I can say it has for me. When I prayed for an opportunity at the division one level I kept working and navigating my way through that path. When my prayers were answered, I was much more prepared and knowledgeable simply because of the opportunities that opened up throughout my journey. What are your thoughts on prayer and failure?

SEASON 5 // FRUSTRATION

"Have we ever thought about including prayer into our journey before we take that leap of faith?"

THOUGHTS

SEASON 5 // FRUSTRATION

"Trust yourself, you know more than you think you do."
— Unknown

I remember when I stepped foot on campus after accepting my dream opportunity. I was nervous for a few days until there was an opportunity when I was required to display knowledge as if I was in that current position for a few years. After exceeding everyone's expectations, my confidence grew.

I then had to have a conversation with myself. How many of us are timid and apprehensive after getting really close to our goal or achieving the goal? We must then make the switch from pursuing to achieved. It's okay to walk a way ... talk a way ... or even have the utmost confidence about yourself and your ability. How can someone tell us we aren't if we know we are?

SEASON 5 // FRUSTRATION

"No matter what the outcome, that's the one thing, besides what I've learned, that can't be taken nor quantified: my experiences."

THOUGHTS

SEASON 5 // FRUSTRATION

"Choose a job you love and you will never have to work a day in your life." — Unknown

What is it that I love to do? That's what I asked myself numerous times when I felt something wasn't right in my life. I enjoyed teaching and having the opportunity to impact students who struggled to defend themselves. I was passionate about the relationships and positive influence I displayed, yet I felt something was missing.

When we have that feeling, what is it that we think is missing? Do we even know what that feeling is? So that poses the question: do we love what we're doing? Or are we doing it simply because it fulfills our financial needs at the moment? If we decide to commit to what it is we desire, we will then never work again. The dedication it takes to pursue what we love alters our lives in more ways than we can imagine. Do we want money or happiness?

SEASON 5 // FRUSTRATION

So that poses the question: do we love what we're doing?"

THOUGHTS

SEASON 5 // FRUSTRATION

"Without patience, one cannot get far in life."
— *Unknown*

How many of us manifested a goal, took that leap of faith, then began to put a timeline on reaching that manifestation? The most detrimental thing we can do while achieving a goal is fooling ourselves into thinking we now control time and can reach that goal whenever we want to. Patience is key. We ingratiate ourselves into the fabric of our journey, appreciating every inch of the process, and learning about each tiny part of ourselves throughout the entire experience. This is what taking that leap of faith embodies.

That's the most important aspect of our manifestation. Allowing ourselves to be patient gives us the time and laser-sharp focus to identify things that need to be fixed, areas that need to be tightened up, as well as strengthening things that can stop us from making a mistake. Is patience one of our strongest traits?

SEASON 5 // FRUSTRATION

"Patience is key. We ingratiate ourselves into the fabric of our journey, appreciating every inch of the process, and learning about each tiny part of ourselves throughout the entire experience. This is what taking that leap of faith embodies."

THOUGHTS

SEASON 5 // FRUSTRATION

"Quit beating yourself up. You're not a finished product. You are still a work in progress." — Unknown

One of the most difficult things I encountered while on my journey is understanding just because things are going well and I'm making progress doesn't mean I know everything. Nor is it an indication that I'm perfect and can't make improvements. We will have success, we will all display leaps and bounds that we've taken, yet there's still so much room to grow. Even after achieving our goal we should be focused on other goals to achieve.

Let's stop being our worst critic. It's a negative outlook on what it is we're trying to do. Champion and constructively criticize yourself, and then focus up and maintain your progression. When we appreciate being a work in progress, that is when we will take that title and find ways to consistently expand on it. When we reach the top of the mountain, are we now a "finished product?" No. We should celebrate for a second, refocus, then begin achieving another goal. We will always be a work in progress. Understanding that displays just how much we understand.

SEASON 5 // FRUSTRATION

"Champion and constructively criticize yourself, and then focus up and maintain your progression."

THOUGHTS

SEASON 5 // FRUSTRATION

"Frustration, although quite painful at times, is a very positive and essential part of success." — Unknown

With understanding being one of the most difficult aspects of my journey, surprisingly frustration was my calm. Why? Because I knew It was coming. I knew I didn't understand everything, thus I was going to make quite a few mistakes. Embody them, know they will come and think about what we can do to counter them. I knew there would be hills I didn't want to climb. So I always wore my climbing shoes. I knew I would be required to know information before I should. So I stayed heavily informed.

What are we doing daily that allows us to limit the time it takes when failing and add that to the time it takes to succeed? Are we not packing a raincoat or umbrella knowing we will see some rain? Or are we searching for shelter while progressing and patiently waiting for those dark clouds? Frustration can only negatively impact our progress if we let it. What are we doing to make sure that's not the deciding factor?

SEASON 5 // FRUSTRATION

"What are we doing daily that allows us to limit the time it takes when failing and add that to the time it takes to succeed?"

THOUGHTS

END OF SEASON 5

Welcome to the end of another great season. Do we look at frustration the same way? What's different about the way we describe it now? And are we much more welcoming to adversity now, or no? I love this season simply because of the negative connotation the word frustration carries. I embraced it. This could have been the single most important thing I did.

Most people sprint as fast as they can from adversity. I looked at it as part of the process. No matter where I turned there would be something that could cause it. A misstep, poor judgment or bad decision could spark a downward cycle of negativity. So keeping a positive attitude and mentality will always alter the time is takes recovering from frustration. This adds to the time it will take for us to achieve our goals. Jot down some of your reactions to frustration. Counter them with what you could try to keep yourself on the path to success.

SEASON 6

Se·ren·i·ty

The state of being calm, peaceful, and untroubled.

SEASON 6 // SERENITY

"Serenity comes when you trade likes for self-worth."
— Unknown

Being in the era of social media, how many of us have allowed the ability to gain acceptance from strangers. Or even fulfill an emptiness within with likes or comments from "friends?" The majority of us, right? How about reaching out for assistance through a tough time, or help in general with making a decision, or concluding something important? I'm guilty! Which one of us would know how to delete those traits just to realize we can do everything we're reaching out to strangers for ourselves?

That's the underlying focus of this book. If we live with ourselves daily, talk to ourselves, know what it is we'd like to do, know how we'd like to accomplish it … then why is it so difficult to block out people who have no idea what we're going through just to motivate ourselves? Imagine if we spent as much time reaching out, accepting, listening and rebutting comments with figuring out how we could get the same result from ourselves. If we can't motivate ourselves, how can we expect someone else to?

SEASON 6 // SERENITY

"Which one of us would know how to delete those traits just to realize we can do everything we're reaching out to strangers for ourselves?"

THOUGHTS

SEASON 6 // SERENITY

"Serenity opens the door to inspiration and creativity."
— *Unknown*

When faced with a difficult challenge, how many of us have closed our eyes, stomped our feet, folded our arms, and made a mean face to get the result we desired? I imagine no one's hand would be raised. So what is it that we could do to assist us in making clear and knowable decisions when faced with a dilemma? Being calm and understanding is yet another hill to climb while mustering up a resourceful rebuttal to adversity.

Allowing ourselves to always be in control limits us from making mistakes that could cost us the time we've spent, efforts we've poured ourselves into, and most importantly an opportunity we've prayed for. Know there is a reason why Serenity falls right after Frustration. They go hand in hand and work in unison. Overcoming frustration opens the door for peace until more adversity arises.

SEASON 6 // SERENITY

"Allowing ourselves to always be in control limits us from making mistakes that could cost us the time we've spent, efforts we've poured ourselves into, and most importantly an opportunity we've prayed for."

THOUGHTS

SEASON 6 // SERENITY

"Don't be afraid to make your mark. Even a tiny ripple can turn into a wave." — Unknown

The "little" things ... who takes the time to focus on the little things that impact our day? A small respectful gesture, a warm welcome, a gracious thank you. Even someone informing us about the information we've regurgitated which could be false, not in a malicious way, but to make sure we don't walk around with inaccurate information. If we all respect those examples, then we should appreciate the small steps we take that gradually develop into leaps towards completing our goals.

Everything we do allows us to gain traction, so never talk yourself out of taking pride in the little things. Remember the journey is where we develop as a person. Everything we do within that journey is a direct reflection on how much we appreciated it. Is there a ripple we've created that transformed into something much more valuable than we expected?

SEASON 6 // SERENITY

"Everything we do allows us to gain traction, so never talk yourslef out of taking pride in the little things. Remember the journey is where we develop as a person. Everything we do within that journey is a direct reflection on how much we appreciated it."

THOUGHTS

SEASON 6 // SERENITY

"There's no need to rush. What's meant for you always arrives right on time." — Unknown

Besides my family, what else do I cherish that's just as valuable? Time. We cannot fast forward, rewind or even pause time. There will be grooves within our journey where we will want to speed it up. And there will be times we want to pause to take a break. There will definitely be situations we want to rewind because the failure we're about to endure sets us back further than we'd like.

Don't rush time. Value it. Find new ways to appreciate it and understand not everyone receives the same amount. So don't squander it. There is someone reading this that if they appreciate their time, they will then gain access to everything they need to reach their destination. I'm a firm believer in the mountains we have to climb, the speed bumps that forces us to slow down and the difficulties we come into contact with are the concrete examples that forces us to either get back on track or the reason why our timing will be perfect.

SEASON 6 // SERENITY

"Don't rush time. Value it. Find new ways to appreciate it and understand not everyone receives the same amount. So don't squander it."

THOUGHTS

SEASON 6 // SERENITY

"In the end, everything will work out. And if it doesn't, then it's not the end yet." — Unknown

I know I'm not the only person who's reached the end of a goal and felt something was missing. What would we do if we feel that way? Would we raddle our brains thinking to the beginning of our journey, focusing on the little things we might have missed? Or would we bypass the feeling just to say we've accomplished the goal?

When I created my website and shirts for my brand, I felt like it wasn't enough. I knew there was something else I could do to spread awareness about my brand. I then created my blog. When I posted daily inspirational quotes and thoughts, a few people chimed in and I was ecstatic. Yet there was something missing. When I decided to take the leap to become an author, I knew writing my first book would fulfill that void of something missing. What aren't we seeing that causes us to question: are we really done after we've raced across the finish line?

SEASON 6 // SERENITY

"Would we raddle our brains thinking to the beginning of our journey, focusing on the little things we might have missed?"

THOUGHTS

SEASON 6 // SERENITY

"Tranquility is a choice. So is anxiety. The entire world around us may be in turmoil. But if we want to be peaceful within, we can be." — Unknown

When our journey begins, there will be distractions altering our focus, noise that desires our attention, and the ringing of our cell phones asking for our time. In those moments we can choose to fold or drown out what's designed to hinder our progress. No matter how hectic everything around us may be, we have the power to silence the chaos, turn up our thoughts, organize our plans, and proceed to be ambitious.

We are in control. If we don't believe so it's because we've allowed the noise of the world to take over our thoughts. #iBetOnMe is about us as an individual. We have the power to reach whatever goal we manifest. What's happening outside we can't control. We have all the control over what's happening in-between our ears. What will we do with it? Settle for chaos or work for tranquility?

SEASON 6 // SERENITY

"#iBetOnMe is about us as an individual. We have the power to reach whatever goal we manifest. What's happening outside we can't control. We have all the control over what's happening in-between our ears."

THOUGHTS

SEASON 6 // SERENITY

"Change is never painful. Only the resistance to change is painful." — Unknown

When we decide to invest in ourselves our lives become better. We will encounter challenges, hardships, failures, and success. Our lives will gain value. Has there been a time when we decided to be insubordinate and ignore the signs telling us there's a way to add true value to our lives? It happens all the time. How many of us regret not listening to the signs?

There are some people who live in constant regret simply because they know the avenue they should turn and walk down, yet they settle for walking straight. Those people gain excitement when talking about or in the presence of what's calling them, yet they religiously leave when it's over just to fall back into their comfort.

Is change that painful? Is the thought of the unknown that frightening that we would rather stay cuddled up in our regret and ignore what we've manifested? Do we know someone like this? Or are we that someone?

SEASON 6 // SERENITY

"There are some people who live in constant regret simply because they know the avenue they should turn and walk down, yet they settle for walking straight."

THOUGHTS

SEASON 6 // SERENITY

"We fear rejection, want attention, crave affection, and dream of perfection." — Unknown

The premise behind this book is to believe in what we manifest. How can we fear what wasn't included or desire what wasn't featured in our manifestation? What are we willing to sacrifice? That's what we have to ask ourselves when on the ledge pondering to take that leap of faith. If we want attention and affection, we have to ask ourselves does that come with our rocky journey, an in-depth learning session about ourselves, and failure after failure until we get it right?

What do we want? If we believe there won't be a multitude of things we have to give up in order to be victorious, begin to think differently. There's a lot that comes with pursuing what we manifest. Finding out what all isn't included could deter us. Yet is what isn't included that important?

SEASON 6 // SERENITY

"If we want attention and affection, we have to ask ourselves does that come with our rocky journey, an in-depth learning session about ourselves, and failure after failure until we get it right?"

THOUGHTS

SEASON 6 // SERENITY

"Let loose of what you can't control. Serenity will be yours." — Unknown

Fear. It's been the driving force to failures for centuries. When will we decide to let go of fear and embrace the unknown? Yes, its something we don't know well, yet we know being stagnant results in not progressing. And most of the time it results in failure. Let go of what is holding you back. Let go of what's hindering you from stepping into that peaceful place we yearn for. Serenity awaits anyone who finally has had enough and wants to see what life can be like when taking that leap of faith, navigating through a tough journey, and coming out the other end successful.

Think about what's currently holding you back. Could it be someone around us? Could it be our thoughts that cast negative dispersions fooling us into thinking we will come up short? Or could it be our environment that doesn't scream we have potential? No matter what it is, silence it. Fight like nothing else matters and prove all the noise wrong. It's going to be a challenge. We're going to have trying times. Yet if success was easy, wouldn't everyone be successful?

SEASON 6 // SERENITY

"Serenity awaits anyone who finally has had enough and wants to see what life can be like when taking that leap of faith, navigating through a tough journey, and coming out the other end successful."

THOUGHTS

SEASON 6 // SERENITY

"Listen. Are you breathing just a little and calling it a life?" — Unknown

When I speak to people about what they're trying to accomplish, when they decided to pursue their manifestation, their answers are very clear and to the point. They're extremely passionate, believable and charismatic. It's like they can grasp what they're dreaming right out of thin air. If we can close our eyes and what we're working so hard for can automatically appear, why do we think it's impossible to achieve those same goals once our eyes open? Are we living every day patiently waiting to close our eyes to dream? Or do we open our eyes and live the dream every day?

SEASON 6 // SERENITY

"What are we doing daily that allows us to limit the time it takes when failing and add that to the time it takes to succeed?"

THOUGHTS

END OF SEASON 6

And there we have it. We've come to the sixth and final season: Serenity. How does the wind feel on our faces? Is the view just as breathtaking as we imagined? What crosses our minds knowing we've achieved the unachievable? And finally, what's next?

Many of us know what it's like to reach this altitude while trying to focus on answering the questions we've mustered up on our climb. Some are focused solely on the knots in our stomachs, configuring a plan to safely get down from this mountain. And very few are still standing patiently at the bottom looking up. With more answers than questions, their feet still stand stationary, their neck in pain from looking up. To walk away or walk forward. That is the question. What decision will we make?

Thank You

To my daughter Aniyah ... I dedicate this book to you. You're the greatest gift I could ever pray for. Your passion to be great at everything you do drives me. Your focus to always being you is what made me take this leap. Your creative ways easily sparked ideas that allowed me to structure my thoughts. Thank you for always allowing it to look like I'm a greater father than I am. I've learned so much from having the opportunity to raise a little girl. Continue to lead, continue to make mistakes, continue to mentor your brother, continue learning from your mother, and most importantly, continue being unapologetically you. I love you.

Jameer ... you're easily the second greatest gift I could have ever prayed for. There is nothing I'm more passionate about than being your father. I cried for a few days when we found out you were a boy. Having the opportunity to do what my father did means the world to me. Thank you for being so smart, so funny, so curious, and always following me around. I vow to be a great leader, a great role model, and a great father. Just as I did, you will make mistakes.

Yet it's about what you do after those mistakes that define you. I love you, son. Thank you.

To my wife ... I'm truly grateful knowing God thought enough of me to bless me with such a wonderful woman. You're the flame that has sparked such a man I didn't believe I could be. You're the calm that quiets all the noise surrounding us, and you're the strength to my being that has allowed me to not only become the man I am today, but become the man you've dreamed of. Thank you for everything. Without you, there truly isn't me. When you decided to take my hand and follow me throughout this journey, I didn't know if you were scared or just as crazy as I was. As I look up today, holding YOUR hand while you're leading us defines just how crazy you are. I love you. Thank you for more than you'd ever know.

To everyone who purchased my book ... there aren't enough thank yous in the world that will show just how appreciative I am. When we decide to take what we've endured, what we've fought through, and what we've accomplished, and display it to the world, it's frightening. And it's humbling, yet warranted. Thank you for riding with me, supporting me and learning about me with me. I hope I was able to return the favor. This book is an inclusive book for a reason. Enjoy your journey, appreciate the ride, learn about yourselves and navigate through with knowledge that a lot us don't have. Self-motivation is defined exactly how it's written. If we can't motivate ourselves, how can we look to someone else to do it? This book is written with words we all know. Sometimes it's about giving our own definition to what it is we've read. We all want success, yet defining success differs from person to person. We all can read, yet what we read carries more weight. It means something different and hits us harder—person to person. My goal is for everyone to read this book and create their own. I did, why can't you?

www.ingramcontent.com/pod-product-compliance
Lightning Source LLC
Chambersburg PA
CBHW051402290426
44108CB00015B/2119